AWESOME FORCES OF NATURE

SHATTERING EARTHQUAKES

Revised and Updated

Louise and Richard Spilsbury

Heinemann
LIBRARY
Chicago, Illinois

www.capstonepub.com
Visit our website to find out
more information about
Heinemann-Raintree books.

To order:

☎ Phone 800-747-4992

🖳 Visit www.capstonepub.com
to browse our catalog and order online.

Edited by Megan Cotugno, Abby Colich, and Andrew Farrow
Designed by Richard Parker
Original illustrations © Capstone Global Library 2004
Illustrated by Geoff Ward
Picture research by Hannah Taylor
Production by Alison Parsons
Originated by Capstone Global Library, Ltd.

Library of Congress Cataloging-in-Publication Data
Spilsbury, Louise.
  Shattering earthquakes / Louise and Richard Spilsbury.
    p. cm. -- (Awesome forces of nature)
  Includes bibliographical references and index.
  ISBN 978-1-4329-3784-3 (hc) -- ISBN 978-1-4329-3791-1
(pb) 1. Earthquakes--Juvenile literature. I. Spilsbury, Richard,
1963- II. Title.
  QE521.3.S657 2010
  551.22--dc22
                    2009037565

Acknowledgements

We would like to thank the following for permission to
reproduce photographs: AP Photo: Bedu Saini, Serambi
Indonesia, 15, John Swart, 19, Koji Sasahara, 5, La Prensa
Grafica, 14, Li Gang, Xinhua, 21, Paul Sakuma, file, 16;
Getty Images: AFP Photo/Jes Aznar, 28, AFP/Filippo
Monteforte, 8, Chien-min Chung, Cover, Galen Rowell,
25, Gary S Chapman, 22, Kevin Schafer, 7, Peter
Macdiarmid, 11, Roger Ressmeyer, 26, Ryan Pyle, 20,
YOSHIKAZU TSUNO, 27; Newscom: DANIEL AGUILAR/
REUTERS, 13, DANILO BALDUCCI/SINTESI/SIPA, 18,
JASON LEE/REUTERS, 4; NOAA: National Geophysical
Data Center, 9, 12, 17; Shutterstock Premier: Masatoshi
Okauchi, 23, Sten Rosenlund, 24

We would like to thank Dr. Ramesh Srivastava for his
invaluable help in the preparation of this book.

Every effort has been made to contact copyright holders of
material reproduced in this book. Any omissions will be
rectified in subsequent printings if notice is given to the
publishers.

All the Internet addresses (URLs) given in this book were valid
at the time of going to press. However, due to the dynamic
nature of the Internet, some addresses may have changed, or
sites may have changed or ceased to exist since publication.
While the author and publisher regret any inconvenience this
may cause readers, no responsibility for any such changes can
be accepted by either the author or the publisher.

Contents

Any words appearing in the text in bold, **like this**, are explained in the glossary.

What Is an Earthquake?

Imagine you are reading at a table. You notice that the clock and your glass are beginning to wobble. Then you hear a rumbling sound, like an airplane flying above the house. Objects in the room rattle and shake more and more. Then, suddenly, your whole room jerks, knocking things off the table and pictures off the walls.

This is how it can feel in an earthquake. An earthquake is when the surface of the Earth moves. The ground under our feet usually feels solid, but during an earthquake it shakes, cracks open, and dips. Most earthquakes are very small and people may only feel a slight trembling under their feet. Others can make cracks in walls and jolt books off shelves. The worst earthquakes in the world cause terrible destruction.

The earthquake on May 12, 2008, in China's Sichuan Province caused massive amounts of damage to buildings and roads.

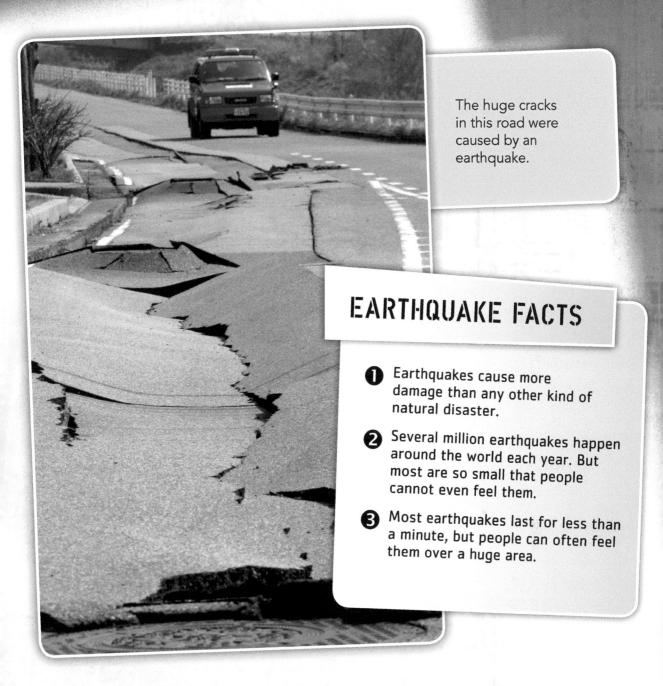

The huge cracks in this road were caused by an earthquake.

EARTHQUAKE FACTS

❶ Earthquakes cause more damage than any other kind of natural disaster.

❷ Several million earthquakes happen around the world each year. But most are so small that people cannot even feel them.

❸ Most earthquakes last for less than a minute, but people can often feel them over a huge area.

Large earthquakes can transform huge areas of the Earth in an instant. During a major earthquake, the shaking of the Earth can knock down buildings, break open roads and bridges, and make huge cracks appear in the land. Cars, buildings, and whole lakes can disappear into these cracks.

5

What Causes Earthquakes?

Earthquakes are movements of the ground. They usually happen in certain places because of the way the Earth is made. To understand how earthquakes happen, you need to know a bit about how our planet is formed.

The surface of the Earth is made of a layer of hard rock. This layer forms the land and the floor of the oceans. It is called the **crust**. Under the crust there is more rock. Millions of years ago, this rock cracked, like the shell of an egg. It split into giant pieces called **plates**. These plates float like huge rafts on hot, liquid rock that bubbles deep inside the Earth. They move very, very slowly around the Earth.

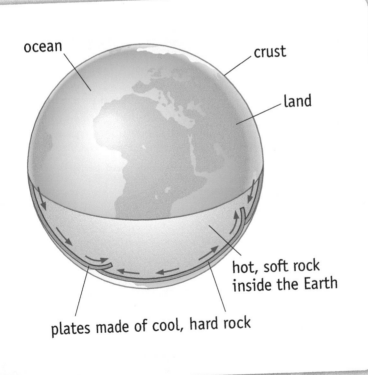

ocean

crust

land

hot, soft rock inside the Earth

plates made of cool, hard rock

The Earth's plates are pieces of rock under the Earth's surface that fit together rather like panels on a soccer ball.

Moving plates

As the plates move, they rub or slide against each other. The place where plates meet is called a **fault**. In most places, one plate slides against another in a slow and steady way. Most plates move at a speed of only a few centimeters each year—that's about the same rate of growth as your fingernails!

Sometimes two plates get stuck against each other. For many years, they slowly push harder and harder against each other. Then, suddenly, the force becomes too much and these gigantic plates of rock slip past each other. When this happens, the crust above shudders and shakes, too. This is an earthquake. The force of the plates suddenly jerking apart can open cracks in the crust above and around the fault.

Fault lines are usually deep underground, but some can be seen on the surface. This is the San Andreas Fault. It runs down the West Coast of North America.

Shock waves

The point on the Earth's surface above the start of an earthquake is called the **epicenter**. The force of an earthquake spreads out in waves from the epicenter in all directions. These movements are called **shock waves**. Shock waves ripple through the rocks all around the epicenter like ripples on a pond when you throw in a stone. Shock waves can travel for hundreds of kilometers, but they get weaker as they get further away from the epicenter.

Aftershocks

Earthquakes usually happen in groups. A major earthquake may start off with small earth **tremors** (movements) that gradually get stronger. These may happen several days before the main earthquake happens. After the main quake, there may be **aftershocks**. Many are too small to feel, but others are like smaller earthquakes. They usually occur within a few days, getting weaker over time.

This damage was caused by the aftershocks that followed a 2009 earthquake in Italy.

Measuring earthquakes

Earthquakes are measured on the **Richter scale**. It is based on the amount of damage they cause. The higher the number on the scale, the more powerful the earthquake is. The weakest earthquake is rated 1 and the strongest earthquake possible would be rated a 10.

What do the ratings mean?

- 2.0 or below: People above ground cannot feel an earthquake like this and it is not recorded.
- Below 4.0: Earthquake can be felt but usually causes little or no damage.
- Over 5.0: Earthquake will be felt by all and could cause some damage.
- Over 6.0: Earthquake that can cause serious damage to buildings.
- Over 7.0: Major earthquake that causes severe damage and can topple buildings over a wide area.
- Over 8.0: Earthquake that causes very severe damage or almost total destruction over a wide area.

On August 17, 1999, an earthquake shook the cities of Izmit and Istanbul in Turkey. It measured 7.4 on the Richter scale and caused terrible damage.

Where Do Earthquakes Happen?

Earthquakes can happen all over the Earth, on land or on the ocean floor. Some earthquakes happen in the middle of **plates**. They happen in places where there is a line of weakness in the Earth's **crust**. But most earthquakes happen where two of the Earth's plates meet.

Many earthquakes happen around the edges of the Pacific Ocean. This is where several plates meet and where hot liquid rock can escape to the surface. This means that many earthquakes and **volcanoes** happen in this area, which has been named the "Ring of Fire." Another area that suffers from many earthquakes is a zone that runs from Italy and Greece, through central Asia and the Himalayas.

This map shows the area where most of the earthquakes on Earth happen.
The red circles mark places where some of the most damaging earthquakes of recent years have happened.
Four out of every five earthquakes occur in the Ring of Fire.

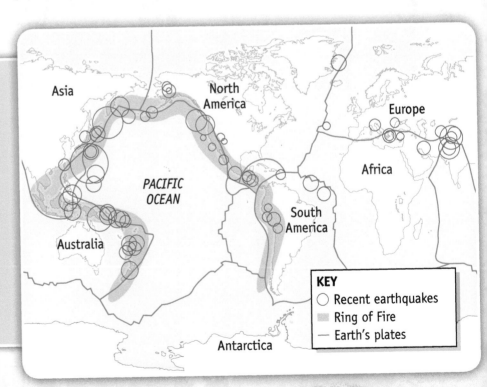

KEY
○ Recent earthquakes
▨ Ring of Fire
— Earth's plates

CASE STUDY

United Kingdom, 2002

Earthquakes can happen in all sorts of places. Few people think of the United Kingdom as an area that has earthquakes. In fact, the United Kingdom has quite a few powerful earthquake every ten years or so. One recent earthquake began at around 1:00 a.m. on September 23, 2002. Thousands of people awoke to feel their houses and furniture shaking and their windows rattling. The earthquake measured 4.8 on the **Richter scale** and its **epicenter** was in Dudley in the West Midlands. It shook buildings in parts of the West Midlands, Wales, North Yorkshire, London, and Wiltshire for up to 30 seconds.

> " *The house started shaking quite violently. All the power was cut off. Quite a few people came out of their houses wondering what was going on. The streets were in darkness.*
>
> —Richard Flynn, West Midlands "

No one was hurt in the West Midlands earthquake, but there was some minor damage.

What Happens in an Earthquake?

Earthquakes usually do most damage at the **epicenter**, but **shock waves** can make land for miles around shake and tremble. In a severe earthquake, the ground can rise and fall like waves in the sea. In the worst cases, the entire shape of the land can be changed.

When an earthquake shakes the ground, it can make walls crack and roofs fall in. If one building falls, it can make the one next to it collapse, too. When earthquakes jolt the ground, they can break electricity cables and gas pipes. Sparks from electricity cables can cause fires and leaking gas can cause explosions. Earthquakes can rip apart roads and crack and bend bridges. **Aftershocks** bring more damage. They make things that were weakened by the first earthquake fall down.

In 1995 an earthquake in Kobe, Japan, killed over 5,000 people. Many people died because the roofs of buildings collapsed on them.

CASE STUDY

Mexico City, 1985

Earthquakes can change landscapes by opening cracks in the Earth and changing land levels. They can also turn firm land into soft, dangerous land.

On September 19, 1985, a huge earthquake hit Mexico City. The epicenter was 50 kilometers (31 miles) off the coast in the sea. However, the quake still rated 8.1 on the **Richter scale** when it reached Mexico City, over 300 kilometers (186 miles) inland. The earthquake was so bad because the city sits on soil made of soft sand and clay. The shock waves shook the soil grains apart, turning it into quicksand. This caused buildings to tilt, shift, or even sink into it. Over 10,000 people were killed, over 40,000 people were injured, and around 100,000 people were left homeless.

Once the dust clouds had cleared, it became obvious that much of Mexico City had been reduced to rubble.

13

Do Earthquakes Cause Other Disasters?

Earthquakes do not just break or bury buildings, bridges, and roads. They can also set off other disasters such as **landslides**. When a hill is damaged and shaken up by an earthquake, the soil on the side of the hill can slide down. This can cause a huge landslide or mudslide. When large amounts of sand or soil fall like this, they can bury people or buildings at the bottom of the hillside.

In 2001 an earthquake rocked El Salvador. It caused a landslide that buried the small town of Las Colinas. The landslide buried hundreds of houses and killed over 450 people.

The town beneath the sea!

In 1692 an earthquake started a landslide in a town called Port Royal on the island of Jamaica. About two-thirds of the town slid into the sea and became buried in the seabed. It was not until 1959 that divers found objects from this lost city on the sea floor.

Earthquakes under the sea

Earthquakes do not only happen on land. They also happen under the sea. When an earthquake happens deep under the water, it creates giant waves called **tsunamis**. Most tsunamis are barely noticeable in deep parts of oceans, but they get bigger as they approach land. When tsunamis hit a coastline they can become like huge walls of water. They sweep away, crush, or flood anything in their path.

The largest earthquake ever recorded measured 9.5 on the **Richter scale**! It struck on May 22, 1960, off the coast of southern Chile, causing terrible damage. It also created a tsunami that caused great destruction all around the Pacific Ocean, especially in Hawaii and Japan.

People wade through water after the tsunami that struck Indonesia in December 2004. The tsunami was caused by an underwater earthquake in the Indian Ocean.

San Francisco, 1989

The city of San Francisco, California, lies on the San Andreas **Fault** and has had several gigantic earthquakes in the past. On October 17, 1989, another huge earthquake hit the city. The **epicenter** was near Santa Cruz, but the earthquake also affected San Francisco and Oakland, 80 kilometers (50 miles) away. It is referred to as the Loma Prieta Earthquake, named for the nearby Loma Prieta Peak.

It was early evening—around 5:00 p.m.—and San Francisco was busy. Many fans were packed into the city's baseball stadium to watch a World Series game. Many city workers were on their way home. The earthquake lasted less than 20 seconds. It rated 7.1 on the **Richter scale**. Around 63 people were killed, over 3,000 were injured, and about $10 billion of damage was caused.

The top deck of this road collapsed onto the lower deck when the earth shook. Cars were crushed, 42 people were killed, and 200 people were injured. This road was later demolished.

Different kinds of damage

There were scenes of destruction all down the Californian coast. In the Santa Cruz mountains, a building slid all the way down a hill. The earthquake also created cracks in the mountainside. One person who lived on the mountain said, "I can't stop shaking. I guess I'm surviving, but I'm scared."

This building was actually shifted onto a car by the immense land movements caused by the Santa Cruz earthquake.

Many roads were cracked or split; **landslides** or rockslides blocked others. Over 90 bridges in the area were damaged, and San Francisco's Bay Bridge was closed for months. Many **mobile homes**, buildings, and businesses were destroyed. Other buildings buckled and bent. The earthquake cracked gas pipes, which led to fires in one area. Water pipes were also damaged so firefighters had to pump seawater from San Francisco Bay to put out the fires.

17

Who Helps After an Earthquake?

Most earthquakes are over in a matter of seconds, but they can cause terrible damage and destruction. The first job after a major earthquake is to rescue survivors and prevent other disasters, such as fires, from causing further damage.

Rescue workers

Firefighters, the army, and **volunteers** all work to rescue people trapped in their homes or cars. They may use specially trained dogs to find people by sniffing them out. Often, rescue workers have to use heavy lifting and cutting equipment to get people out from under crushed buildings or fallen bridges. Damage to buildings and roads after an earthquake may make emergency work more difficult. For example, blocked roads stop firefighters from reaching fires. Construction workers may have to bring cranes and bulldozers to clear roads first. Rescue work is very dangerous because **aftershocks** can be devastating, too.

These rescue workers are searching for survivors after an earthquake in L'Aquila, Italy, in April 2009.

After an earthquake, workers have to clear up the rubble from wrecked buildings and roads. They also check that any buildings left standing are safe enough for people to move back in to.

Helping people

Ambulances try to arrive at the scene as quickly as possible. Ambulance staff give emergency medical treatment and take injured people to the hospital. Workers from the Red Cross and other **aid organizations** also help after earthquakes. As well as giving **first aid**, they provide people whose homes have been destroyed with somewhere to stay and food to eat.

The work does not stop after everyone has been rescued or taken to the hospital. New homes have to be built for people who have lost their homes. Aid organizations help people who have become separated from their families to find them again. People may have also lost their businesses or shops. Often ordinary people send money to help earthquake victims rebuild their lives.

CASE STUDY

China, 2008

The afternoon of May 12, 2008, turned tragic as an earthquake blasted through the Sichuan province of central China. At 2:28 p.m., a quake that measured 7.9 on the **Richter scale** rocked this mountainous region from the **epicenter** in Wenchuan County. It killed nearly 70,000 people, making it one of the deadliest earthquakes of all time.

It lasted for almost three minutes, crumbling buildings miles away. **Tremors** were felt as far away as Russia and Pakistan. **Aftershocks** continued for months, causing further damage and more deaths. Hundreds of thousands of people were injured and millions were left homeless.

A boy walks among the devastation caused by the May 12, 2008, earthquake in China. Tens of thousands were killed in the disaster.

Schoolchildren deaths

Many of the people who died during the earthquake were schoolchildren. Buildings in China are supposed to be strong enough to withstand an earthquake. But many schools were built with materials that were not strong enough.

Some parents of the children killed tried to speak out. They wanted answers from the government about why the schools were built with such poor materials. A year later, the Chinese government said it would spend extra money making new schools safer.

This boy was trapped when his school building collapsed in the earthquake of 2008. He was one of the lucky few to be rescued.

Can Earthquakes Be Predicted?

It is very hard to tell when and where an earthquake will happen. Sometimes there are small **tremors** first. Often, animals behave oddly before an earthquake—dogs bark wildly, horses rear up, and snakes, mice and rats come out of their holes. However, these things do not always happen. Even if they do, it may be too close to the actual earthquake for there to be enough time to escape.

Studying earthquakes

Scientists who study earthquakes are called **seismologists**. They use machines called **seismometers** to measure shaking of the ground. They gather information from thousands of seismometers all around the world. Using maps that show where the world's **faults** are, seismologists study slight movements of the ground. If there is more shaking and ground movement than usual, an earthquake is more likely.

This seismograph is creating a chart. The lines indicate where the ground has moved. The larger the line, the more movement from the ground.

Seismometers provide useful information about an earthquake as it happens. But scientists are also working on ways of predicting earthquakes. One way is using information collected by **satellites** above the Earth. Special cameras in the satellites measure the shape of the Earth's **crust**. These measurements show if there are small changes that could warn of an earthquake. Scientists hope that this information will be able to help them to predict some earthquakes in the future.

This scientist is using a computer to monitor earthquake activity in Tokyo, Japan. Predicting earthquakes is a hope for the future.

A success story

A warning to **evacuate** was given to the people of Haicheng in China several days before a bad earthquake in 1975. There had been several warning signs, including animals behaving oddly, land shifting, water seeping out of the ground, and small tremors. When these tremors got stronger, the warning was given and many lives were saved. Unfortunately, most earthquakes do not give such clear warning signals.

Can People Prepare for Earthquakes?

At present it is almost impossible to predict that an earthquake is definitely going to happen. The best way to reduce the amount of damage earthquakes cause is for everyone to be well prepared.

Making buildings safer

One of the greatest causes of death in an earthquake is people being crushed under buildings. One of the main ways of saving lives is to build homes and other buildings that are strong enough to cope with earthquakes. Even in the strongest quakes, these should at least stay standing long enough for people to escape. Designers create buildings that can move slightly in an earthquake without breaking up.

In the Loma Prieta earthquake in 1989, the Transamerica Pyramid in San Francisco shook badly. However, the building was not damaged and no one was hurt. This 48-story office building has special supports at its base that protect it from the ground-shattering effects of earthquakes.

One way of strengthening mud buildings like these in Peru is to join edges with a mesh of wire and cover them with concrete. However, even this cheap solution costs too much for many people.

The most important thing builders have to consider is the land they are about to build on. Tall buildings should never be placed on loose soil that might sink and shift in an earthquake. When people make bridges or office buildings with metal frames, they should include rubber pads to absorb the **shocks** of an earthquake. This allows the building to move slightly with the shaking, rather than breaking up.

What about poorer countries?

Unfortunately, many earthquakes happen in places where people cannot afford to pay for safety measures like these. Poorer people may have no choice about the materials with which they build their homes. In Peru millions of people live in cheap **adobe** (mud) houses. These often fall down in earthquakes because the walls are not connected together and mud is a weak building material.

How should people prepare?

People who live in earthquake zones should not worry about earthquakes. But everyone in the family should learn exactly what to do. They should all know how to **evacuate**. They should know a safe place to go to and a safe route to get there. Local government offices can give people information about what to do in an earthquake.

Things to do to prepare

There are several ways people can make the insides of their homes safer. Things that can fall, break, or start fires may injure people. So people should bolt or strap heaters, cupboards, and bookcases to walls to stop them from falling. It is also a good idea to keep heavy objects on the bottom shelves, and to hang pictures and mirrors away from beds.

This team is reinforcing the basement of a house so it can withstand earthquakes better.

What to do in an earthquake

One way of being prepared is knowing what to do in an earthquake. Here are some tips to remember:

- Try not to panic. Earthquakes are scary, but they usually only last a few seconds.

- If you are indoors, take cover immediately under a strong table or desk. Stay away from glass, windows, or anything that could fall, like a bookcase.

- If you are outdoors, move away from buildings, street lights, telephone wires, and **power lines**.

- If you are in a crowded place, don't rush for the doors if everyone else is doing that. Never get into an elevator.

- Don't forget that there may be **aftershocks** following an earthquake. Aftershocks can cause things that were weakened by the main earthquake to fall down.

These students in Japan are practicing an earthquake drill. One of the most important things to remember during an earthquake is to protect yourself from falling objects.

Haiti, 2010

Haiti, in the Caribbean, is located on the boundary between two of the earth's **plates**, the North American plate and the Caribbean plate. At 4:53 p.m. on Tuesday, January 12, 2010, a massive earthquake struck Haiti. The magnitude of the earthquake measured 7.0 on the **Richter scale**. It was the worst earthquake to hit the area in over 200 years. The **epicenter** was only 15 kilometers (10 miles) from the capital of Haiti, Port-au-Prince.

The following day the devastation caused by the earthquake became clear. Government buildings, hospitals, and many homes were completely destroyed by the earthquake and its powerful **aftershocks**. It is believed that around 200,000 people may have died. Countries from around the world, including the U.S. and China, immediately began to send rescue teams and medical supplies to help the people of Haiti.

Five days after the earthquake struck, survivors walk through the wreckage of the market area in Port-au-Prince, Haiti.

CASE STUDY

Christchurch, New Zealand, 2011

The people of New Zealand are used to earthquakes—the country experiences thousands every year. The quakes are almost always small, however, with little damage and effect on people's lives. Tuesday, February 22, 2011, was different. That afternoon a powerful earthquake struck Christchurch on New Zealand's South Island. The earthquake measured 6.3 on the Richter scale. It was very damaging because it occurred close to the surface and near a major city.

Christchurch is New Zealand's second largest city, with almost 400,000 people. The earthquake struck during the busy weekday lunch hour, making the disaster worse. Streets cracked open and many buildings collapsed. Rescue workers fought to free survivors who were trapped under rubble and overturned vehicles. More than 180 people died from the earthquake. It was New Zealand's worst natural disaster since an earthquake that struck the North Island in 1931.

New Zealand suffers many small quakes every year, but the Christchurch earthquake of 2011 was New Zealand's worst natural disaster since a 1931 earthquake.

Glossary

adobe clay used to make bricks that are dried in the sun

aftershock small tremors or ground movements that happen soon after the main jolt of an earthquake

aid organizations groups of people who work together to raise money and to provide help for people in need

crust layer of rock that forms the land we live on and the floor of the oceans

epicenter point on the Earth's surface above the start of an earthquake

evacuate/evacuation when people move from a dangerous place to somewhere they will be safe

fault place where two or more different plates meet below the Earth's crust

first aid first medical help given to injured people

landslides when heavy rains and wind make large amounts of mud and rock slide down a hill or mountain

mobile home home that can be moved

plates the rocky layer that forms the surface of the Earth is split into giant pieces. These pieces are called plates.

power lines main cables that carry electricity

Richter scale scale that tells people how powerful an earthquake is

satellite object that goes around the Earth in space. Satellites do jobs such as sending out TV signals or taking photographs.

scientist person who studies aspects of the world around us

seismologist scientist who studies earthquakes

seismometer machine that measures the shaking of the ground

shock violent shaking movement caused by an earthquake

shock waves movements through the ground caused by an earthquake. Shock waves ripple through rocks all around the epicenter like ripples on a pond.

tremor shaking of the ground

tsunami giant wave caused by an earthquake or other disturbance, such as a landslide

volcano when hot liquid rock from the center of the Earth spurts out from a hole in the Earth's crust

volunteers people who work without being paid for what they do

Find Out More

Books

Colson, Mary. *Shaky Ground: Earthquakes*. (Chicago: Raintree, 2006).

Farndon, John. *Predicting Earthquakes*. (Chicago: Heinemann Library, 2009).

Tagliaferro, Linda. *How Does an Earthquake Become a Tsunami?* (Chicago: Raintree, 2009).

Townsend, John. *Earthquakes and Volcanoes: A Survival Guide*. (Chicago: Raintree, 2006).

Websites

Earthquakes for Kids
http://earthquake.usgs.gov/learning/kids
A website about earthquakes produced by the U.S. Geological Survey. It contains science projects, facts and pictures.

FEMA for Kids
www.fema.gov/kids/quake.htm
The FEMA website for kids contains useful facts about what an earthquake is, earthquake dangers, what to do and how to prepare.

Weather Wiz Kids
www.weatherwizkids.com/weather-earthquake.htm
Visit this website to find out more about how earthquakes work.

Index